Nineteenth-Century
EUROPEAN
PIANO MUSIC
Unfamiliar Masterworks

Selected and Introduced by

JOHN GILLESPIE
Professor of Music, University of California

Dover Publications, Inc.
New York

CONTENTS

Published in Canada by General Publishing Company, Ltd., 30 Lesmill Road, Don Mills, Toronto, Ontario.
Published in the United Kingdom by Constable and Company, Ltd., 10 Orange Street, London WC 2.

Nineteenth-Century European Piano Muisc is a new collection of music, selected and introduced by John Gillespie and first published by Dover Publications, Inc., in 1977. The individual original publications here reprinted are indicated in the table of contents.

International Standard Book Number: 0-486-23447-9
Library of Congress Catalog Card Number: 76-28935

Manufactured in the United States of America
Dover Publications, Inc.
180 Varick Street
New York, N.Y. 10014

INTRODUCTION

Every age has its distinguishing manner or mood, but this dominating style is always softened by stylistic elements carried over from other eras. The nineteenth century is generally referred to as the Romantic era. In an intellectual and artistic rebellion against the rules and restraints imposed on thought and art during the Classic period, nineteenth-century writers, philosophers, composers and artists strove for originality, avoiding everything related to convention and tradition.

Absorbed with man's personal emotions and desires, Romantic composers emphasized the subjective, the natural and the fantastic, yet intended that their free inspiration should be governed by universal rules of form and structure. These composers favored the piano, for that instrument, equally at home in the salon or on the concert stage, could convey their innermost feelings as well as their outright emotions. Although piano sonatas were written during the Romantic era, most composers preferred the étude, theme and variations, stylized dances—like the waltz and polka—and other free forms, such as the fantasy, arabesque and nocturne. To be effective most of these free forms depended on contrasting themes; however, composers frequently neglected formal thematic development.

The Romantic era produced innumerable short, distinctive works created especially for the piano: idiomatic, musical epigrams, which in some ways are instrumental counterparts of the vocal lied and art song. The so-called character piece, therefore, developed as the favorite keyboard form during the nineteenth century. It was most often in ternary form (A B A), whether two pages or twelve pages long. Beyond this basic formal outline, the composer could release his imagination and inspiration to embellish the framework.

Chopin, Liszt, Schumann, Brahms and Mendelssohn are outstanding names in the field of nineteenth-century piano music, but there were many other composers—some very well known and some of lesser reputation—who also fashioned excellent piano music that deserves to be studied and performed. For that reason, this anthology offers both pianist and listener an opportunity to explore some of the unusual, less frequently heard piano music from the Romantic era.

Musical quality was the most important requisite in choosing the compositions. With that established, works were selected from the following categories: piano music by composers primarily known for works in other media, piano music by less familiar composers, and music not often found in anthologies.

THE COMPOSERS

Isaac Albéniz (1860–1909), b. Spain. A prolific composer, Albéniz is best known for his dazzling, picturesque and thoroughly refined piano music. Not a true Romantic in the sense that Chopin and Schumann were Romantics, he described in his music more of what he saw than what he felt. Emotionally he was a more objective composer than his Spanish contemporaries, but like them he drew inspiration from the natural beauties of his homeland and the vividly dramatic temperament of his own people. *España*, Op. 165 (1890), a collection of six compositions with genuine Spanish flavor, clearly reveals the basic characteristics of Albéniz' art: objectivity and realism.

Anton Arensky (1861–1906), b. Russia. In general Arensky's music is suavely lyric and tends to be eclectic rather than nationalistic. Although many of his works show a strong Tchaikovsky influence, Arensky depended more on technical skill than emotional inspiration. Outside of his native Russia his reputation rests largely on his music for two pianos. The middle section of the Etude, Op. 25, No. 3, is built around a pentatonic melody that Arensky describes as a *thème chinois*.

Agathe Backer-Grøndahl (1847–1907), b. Norway. In her own time this pianist-composer was greatly admired for her songs and epigrammatic piano compositions. These typically small-scale works indicate that a fertile musical imagination combined with a skillful technique enabled her to express romantic feeling without sentimentality. *Fantasistykker* (Fantasy Pieces), Op. 45, consists of five compositions representative of her style: "Song of Youth," "Zephyr," "Summer Song," "Swinging" and "Waltz."

Mily Balakirev (1837–1910), b. Russia. Balakirev was leader of The Five, a group of ardent nationalist composers who helped to set the course of Russian music during the second half of the nineteenth century. For inspiration he turned to Russian folk music and the music of the Romantic composers of Western Europe, notably Liszt. Balakirev's large piano repertoire includes the inordinately difficult Oriental fantasy *Islamey* and the highly characteristic Scherzo in B-flat Minor, which has been chosen for this anthology. The Scherzo, written at the very end of the nineteenth century, is an extended work of elegant virtuosity.

Georges Bizet (1838–1875), b. France. An inborn musical talent and long years of training at the Paris Conservatory earned Bizet the Prix de Rome when he was only eighteen, with the result that he spent nearly three happy years writing and studying in that city. Although famous primarily as a composer of operas (especially *Carmen*), Bizet wrote two important keyboard works: *Jeux d'enfants* (Children's Games, 1871), a piano duet, and *Variations chromatiques* (1868), his finest solo keyboard composition. In the highly imaginative variations the theme is based on an ascending and descending chromatic scale.

Alexander Borodin (1833-1887), b. Russia. Borodin devoted his life to two masters, science and music, and unfortunately the demands of his successful career as a chemist left too little time for his work as a composer. A dedicated nationalist, he sought musical inspiration in Russian folksong and the rich Oriental influences absorbed from the neighboring East, both sources being well suited to his lyrical, heroic style. Although Borodin found time to compose only a small body of works, the Symphony in B Minor, the remarkable opera *Prince Igor*, the two String Quartets and the songs are of such quality and importance that they rank as masterpieces of Russian music. His one significant piano work, included here, is the *Petite Suite* (1885), a collection of seven short compositions—the tranquil "In the Monastery," "Intermezzo," two spirited "Mazurkas," "Serenade," "Nocturne," "Rêverie"—followed by an extended "Scherzo."

Emmanuel Chabrier (1841–1894), b. France. Having dutifully taken a degree in law, Chabrier spent eighteen unenthusiastic years working in the Ministry of the Interior, all the while finding his greatest pleasure in composing and in the company of artistic friends. When in 1880 he finally resigned from the Ministry to devote full time to a musical career, he was not taken too seriously until successful performances of his works in Germany led to recognition at home. Chabrier's music, intrinsically interesting and historically significant because it contains the germs of Impressionism, sparkles with vitality, fantasy and rhythmic energy. This energy is especially prominent in the comparatively few piano compositions that he wrote, for example, the whimsical Impromptu and the intriguing rondo entitled "Ronde champêtre."

MUZIO CLEMENTI (1752–1832), b. Italy. Clementi's innate musical ability, early childhood instruction and years of study in England prepared him well for his eminent career as pianist and composer. Intuitively understanding the differences between the piano and the harpsichord, he developed a writing style to exploit the piano's natural characteristics. As a composer he is remembered chiefly for the more than sixty piano sonatas he composed and the *Gradus ad Parnassum* (1817), an enduring collection of one hundred studies in pianistic dexterity, many of which possess unusual artistic merit and compare favorably with Chopin's études. The *Suite de quatre pièces* from the *Gradus* consists of four compositions typical of Clementi's style—an energetic Preludio, a skillfully designed Fuga, a lyrical Adagio sostenuto and a virtuoso Finale.

CARL CZERNY (1791-1857), b. Austria. At the age of ten Czerny was accomplished enough in music to have Beethoven accept him as a pupil, and during the next three years his playing advanced rapidly under the master's disciplined teaching and paternal friendship. At the same time, the amazingly vigorous and talented child put just as much effort into the study of composition. Never eager to perform in public, Czerny retired rather early from the concert stage—and from society in general—choosing to devote his enormous energies to composing and teaching. Hummel, whose playing astonished him, and Clementi, whose teaching method he studied, both influenced his writing style. In this anthology, "Chanson sans paroles," Op. 795, No. 1, and "Etude mélodieuse," Op. 795, No. 3, show him to good advantage as a composer of lyrical music, and the Toccata in C Major, Op. 92, substantiates his reputation as an expert composer of technically demanding music.

JAN LADISLAV DUSÍK (Johann Ladislaus Dussek; 1760–1812), b. Czechoslovakia. Already established as a composer, performer and teacher, Dusík arrived in Hamburg at the age of twenty-three and arranged to take further studies with Carl Philipp Emanuel Bach. With encouragement from Bach, Dusík by the following year had begun a lifelong career that took him throughout Europe and England giving concerts, composing and teaching, usually under the generous patronage of a noble or affluent person. One of the most important keyboard composers of his day, he wrote some fifty piano sonatas which contain various stylistic elements that later found fulfillment in Beethoven, Schubert, Chopin, Weber, Schumann, Liszt and even Brahms. Dusík's outstanding piano works, however, are the Sonata in F Minor, Op. 77, and (included here) the Sonata in A-flat Major, Op. 70, which is a masterpiece in style, form and harmony.

ANTONÍN DVOŘÁK (1841–1904), b. Czechoslovakia. Many critics place Dvořák in the front rank of nineteenth-century symphonists. He learned about the orchestra while playing viola in the National Theater Orchestra in Prague from 1862 until 1873, a period when he also worked steadily at composing. Johannes Brahms, recognizing unique creativity in Dvořák's talent, helped him to get his works published, so that eventually he was able to leave the orchestra and give more time to composing. The natural freshness of his music—born of his spontaneous inspiration and creative imagination—can be seen in the six *Silhouettes* from Op. 8 (1879).

GABRIEL FAURÉ (1845–1924), b. France. Fauré might be described as a nineteenth-century classicist whose main concern was balance between content and form. Rather than attempting to create new expressive modes or technical devices, he accepted contemporary aesthetics and regarded himself as the logical product of a long-established tradition. His classic roots were formed during his early student years at the Ecole Niedermeyer, where he received strong doses of J. S. Bach. From Saint-Saëns he learned the essentially French precepts of clarity and unity, but in his own music he enveloped them in his predominantly Romantic spirit. The harmony in his piano music is often linear. In other instances, particularly the later keyboard works, strict economy of notes results in a simple, sometimes austere, chordal structure. Swiftly moving modulations, subtle chromaticisms and an easy-flowing grace in the melodic line all contribute to this aristocratic music, which is the essence of French *sensibilité*. The *Theme and Variations*, Op. 73 (1897), is one of the finest sets of variations written in the nineteenth century.

JOHN FIELD (1782–1837), b. Ireland. Apprenticed to Clementi at an early age and one of his favorite pupils, Field ultimately spent thirty years in St. Petersburg and Moscow as a soloist and teacher. His greatest fame now lies not in his music or excellent reputation as a pianist but in the form of nocturne that he originated and Chopin later glorified: a short elegy of great lyric intensity. In Field's classic model, a simple melody with harmonic accompaniment, it is easy to find the details that must have appealed to Chopin: the dreamy, atmospheric and usually nostalgic mood of the nocturne, and the coloratura passages that occasionally interrupt the melodic line. Nocturne No. 2 in C Minor, though brief, contains the essence of these characteristics. Nocturne No. 4 in A Major, with its variety and wide-ranging emotions, is possibly Field's finest nocturne.

NIELS GADE (1817–1890), b. Denmark. Gade is Denmark's most famous nineteenth-century composer. Following a term as violinist in the Royal Orchestra of Copenhagen, he studied at Leipzig, where Mendelssohn befriended him and for several years shared with him the conducting of the Leipzig Gewandhaus concerts. When he returned to Copenhagen, Gade established himself as an organist and conductor. Much of his music is nationalistic, but the influence of the years spent with Mendelssohn is forcefully present in the four sections of the *Arabeske*, Op. 27 (1854). These compositions are designed to be played consecutively without pause; however, the first three may be played separately by omitting the connecting passages at the end of each piece.

ENRIQUE GRANADOS (1867–1916), b. Spain. Granados enjoyed a life full of success in composing, performing and teaching. As a composer he has been criticized for being less "Spanish" in his music than some of his contemporaries, but his subjective approach carried his music beyond the limits of actual Hispanicism. His nationalism served only as a basic outline, a means to an end, and with this approach he composed some of the sublimest piano music ever written on the Spanish peninsula. The four dance collections *Danzas españolas* (Spanish Dances, 1893) show refined elegance and noble character rather than the homely feeling of imitation folk music. Of the twelve compositions in these collections, four are included in this anthology.

STEPHEN HELLER (1814–1888), *b.* Hungary. A pianist-composer, Heller studied in Vienna, toured Europe extensively and eventually settled in Paris, where he became identified with the circle of composers—Chopin, Liszt, Berlioz and others—then residing in that city. Like Chopin he wrote almost exclusively for piano—sonatas, fantasias, studies, characteristic pieces. Robert Schumann admired Heller's music, believing that "he generally feels naturally and expresses himself clearly and cleverly." The *Three German Dances* included here are short and idiomatic. Equally brief, the Toccatina is alternately piquant and lyrical.

JOHANN NEPOMUK HUMMEL (1778–1837), *b.* Czechoslovakia. Mozart, seldom keenly enthusiastic about a piano student, found Hummel to be such a rare exception that he took him into his home, taught him and presented him in a concert. As the boy progressed from student to performer and composer, he had more good fortune in receiving lessons and advice from such masters as Haydn, Salieri, Clementi and Albrechtsberger. With his inherent gift for improvisation and his sensitive interpretations of other composers' works as well as his own, Hummel was a marvelous success on the concert stage. His *Pianoforte School* (1828) was a valuable contribution to the art of piano playing, and many of his keyboard compositions are highly attractive. The *Variations on a Theme from "Armide" by Gluck*, Op. 57, exploit a multifaceted keyboard technique through ten expertly designed variations.

IGNAZ MOSCHELES (1794–1870), *b.* Czechoslovakia. An excellent pianist as well as a composer, Moscheles earned a formidable reputation for his superb technique and clear, incisive touch. During his lifetime his piano compositions were also much appreciated, and some of them still merit study and performance. Moscheles' most carefully written keyboard works are the three *Allegri di bravura*, Op. 51, *Twenty-four Etudes*, Op. 70, and *Characteristische Studien*, Op. 95. "La Forza" from Op. 51 is indeed a bravura allegro, accomplished with elaborate flourish and dramatic feeling.

BEDŘICH SMETANA (1824–1884), *b.* Czechoslovakia. Although better known for his colorful orchestral tone poems, like *The Moldau*, Smetana is also an important keyboard composer. As a performer he was a competent pianist who followed Liszt in matters of technique, and as a composer he was a strong nationalist who searched Chopin's music to find ways to utilize his own country's cultural heritage. The *Bagatelles* and *Impromptus* written in 1844 are his first wholly personal expressions in music. That Smetana achieved for the polka what Chopin had accomplished for the mazurka is well illustrated by the Polka in E-flat Major, Op. 8, No. 1, and the "Venkovanka," both reprinted here.

RICHARD STRAUSS (1864–1949), *b.* Germany. The music of Richard Strauss, which at various times suggests the influence of Brahms, Liszt and Wagner, pursues the Romantic mystique to its utmost limits. Strauss was born with an exceptional ability for descriptive writing, and since that style is better suited to symphonic poems and operas, he composed very few keyboard works. Those he did produce—like the delightful *Stimmungsbilder*, Op. 9 (1883) —were written early in his career. Two compositions from this collection—"In Silent Forests" and "Intermezzo"— appear in this anthology. Although they are early works, they contain definite indications of Strauss's more mature style.

VÁCLAV JAN TOMÁŠEK (Johann Wenzel Tomaschek; 1774– 1850), *b.* Czechoslovakia. Educated in law and philosophy but by nature inclined to music, Tomášek hesitated between a career in music and a civil career. Having mastered the fundamental rules of composition—he was largely self-taught in music—he became a proficient and fruitful composer. Beethoven and Haydn were his friends, but among composers he preferred Mozart. Tomášek's personal style is sharpest in his piano music and songs— a romantic, lyrical style that affected the works of John Field and Franz Schubert and laid a foundation for Smetana. Tomášek's short, poetic pianoforte works are direct harbingers of the Romantic age. The Dithyramb in C Minor, the first of the three *Ditirambi*, Op. 65 (1818), is an intensely dramatic, compelling poem. (The composer's middle name in its Czech form is sometimes given as Jaromir instead of Jan.)

JAN HUGO VOŘÍŠEK (Johann Hugo Worzischek; 1791– 1825), *b.* Czechoslovakia. Voříšek went to Vienna in 1813, ostensibly to read law but actually to cultivate Beethoven's friendship, and there he found his way into the circle that included Moscheles, Hummel and Meyerbeer. Like his teacher Tomášek, Voříšek tended toward lyricism, and he was one of the finest overt Romanticists to work in Vienna. His *Impromptus*, Op. 7 (1822), had an effect on similar works by Schubert; in ternary form, they contrive to evoke both mood and acute, intimate feeling— all within a few pages. Impromptu No. 2 in G major is reprinted here.

RICHARD WAGNER (1813–1883), *b.* Germany. Wagner, a robust, romantic, expansive man, dedicated his career to creating an art form in which music, drama and spectacle were unified into one grandiose production—the Wagnerian opera. Whatever problems he experienced in creating this unique genre were overshadowed by his instinctive musicianship, melodic talent, harmonic inventiveness and masterly orchestration. In his operas Wagner achieved what he believed, that music is not meant to be logically examined but is a power of nature that men can perceive but do not understand. He worked with a few other forms besides the massive operas, and so far as the piano works are concerned they must be generally described as salon music. A notable exception, the one-movement *Album-Sonate* (1853), qualifies as a serious composition.

ACKNOWLEDGMENT

Editor and publisher are most grateful to the library system of the University of California for lending all the music for reproduction. Special thanks are due to Ms. Marsha Berman, Music Librarian, Music Library, Schoenberg Hall, University of California, Los Angeles; Dr. Vincent Duckles, Head, Music Library, The General Library, University of California, Berkeley; and to the coordinator of the loan, Mr. Martin Silver, Music Librarian, The Arts Library, University of California, Santa Barbara.

ESPAÑA

SIX FEUILLES D'ALBUM

J. ALBENIZ

Nº 1. PRÉLUDE

Nº 2 . TANGO

J. ALBENIZ

Nº 3. MALAGUEÑA

J. ALBENIZ

Nº 4 _ SERENATA

J. ALBENIZ

Nº 5. CAPRICHO CATALAN

J. ALBENIZ

España: Capricho catalan 19

Nº 6_ ZORTZICO

J. ALBENIZ

À Monsieur S. RÉMÉZOFF.

ETUDE.

A. ARENSKY. Op.25.Nº3.

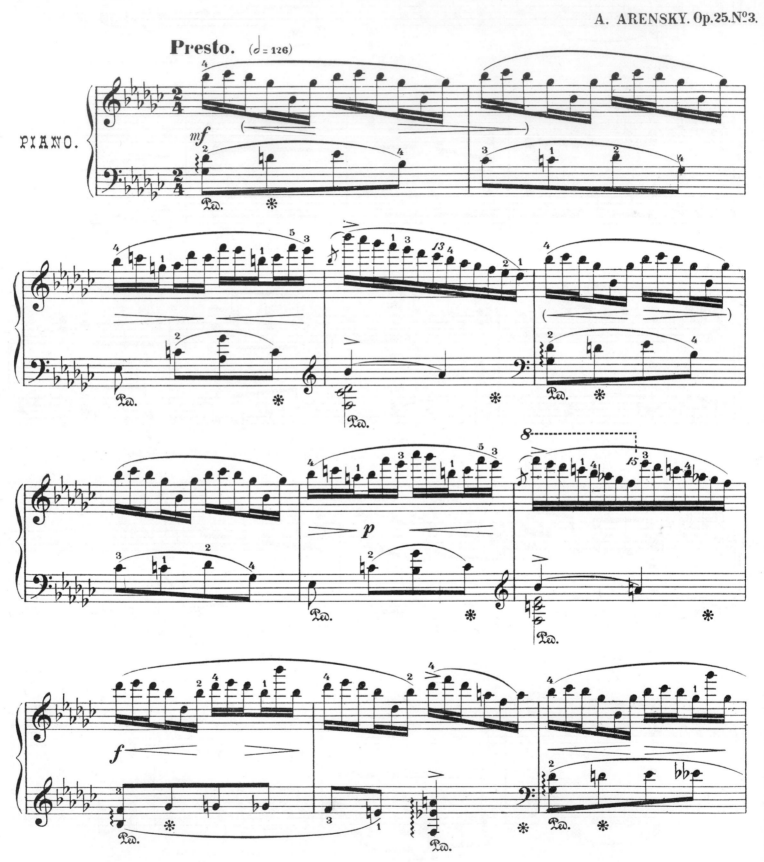

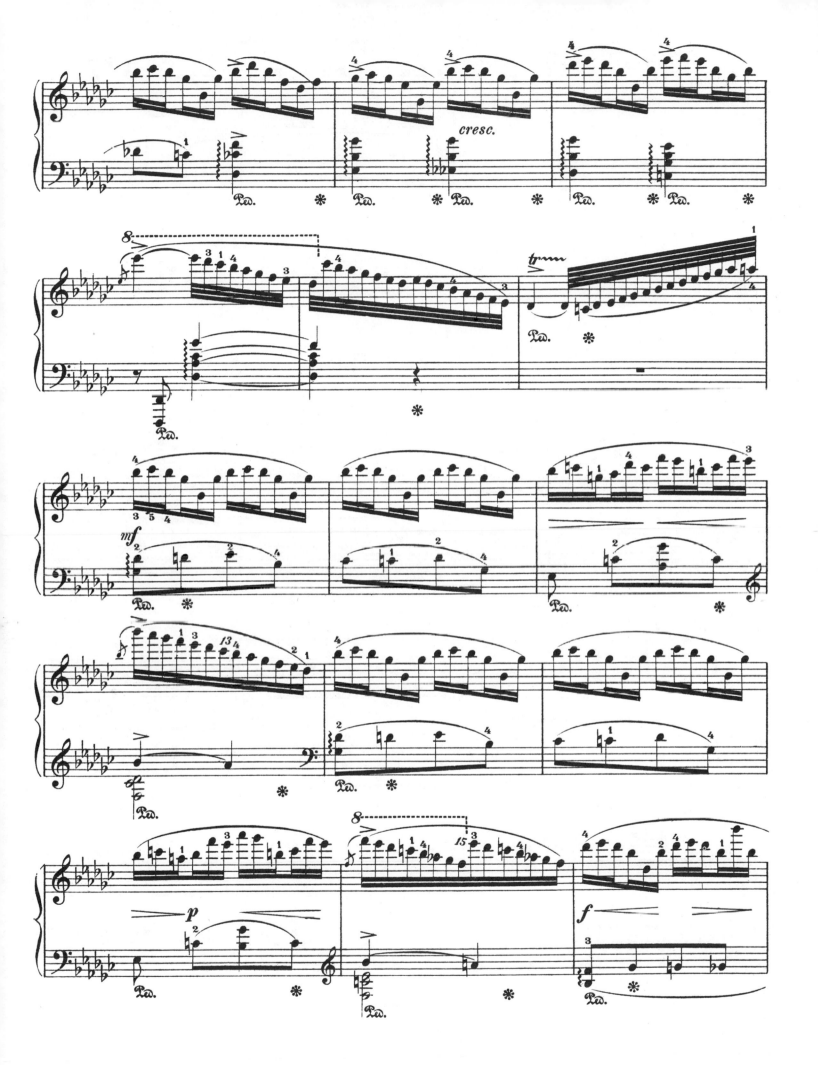

Thême chinois.

UNGDOMSSANG.

Agathe Backer Gröndahl, Op. 45 № 1.

ZEPHYR.

Agathe Backer Gröndahl, Op. 45 № 2.

Agathe Backer Grøndahl

SOMMERVISE.

Agathe Backer Gröndahl, Op. 45 No 3.

Andantino semplice. M.M. ♪ = 116.

GYNGENDE.

Agathe Backer Gröndahl, Op. 45 No 4.

Allegretto non troppo.

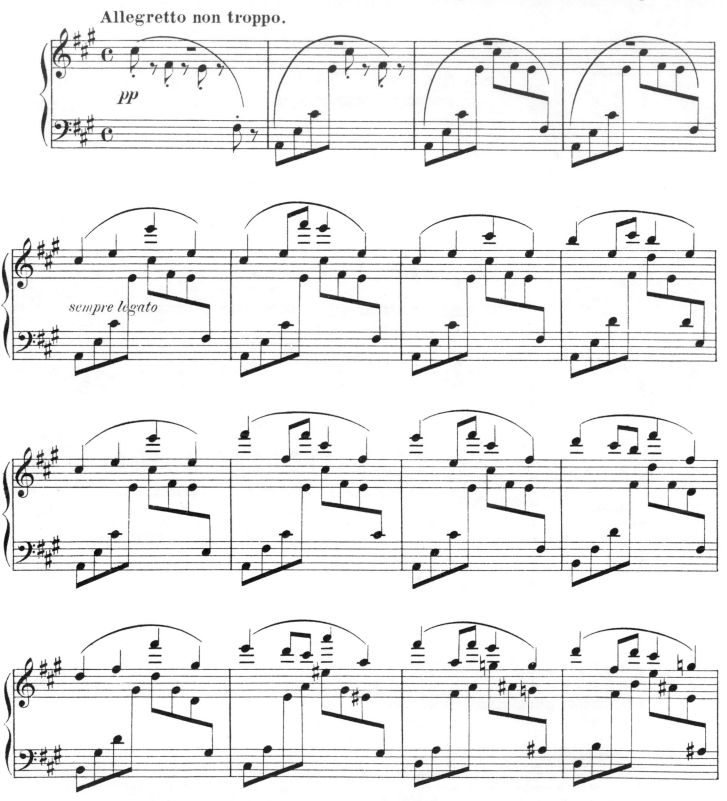

VALS.

Agathe Backer Gröndahl, Op.45 N°5.

Molto con anima. ♩.= 96.

SECOND SCHERZO

Allegro moderato
Quasi corno

(29/VI 1900)

VARIATIONS

CHROMATIQUES.

GEORGES BIZET.

À STEPHEN HELLER

(EDITION DE CONCERT)

VAR. 2.

VAR. 3.
a tempo risoluto.

VAR. 4.
Con fuoco.

ff très rhythmé et martelé.

Ped. *

très rhythmé et martelé: very rhythmic and hammered out

le trémolo très serré: very rapid tremolo

le chant bien marqué: bring out the melody

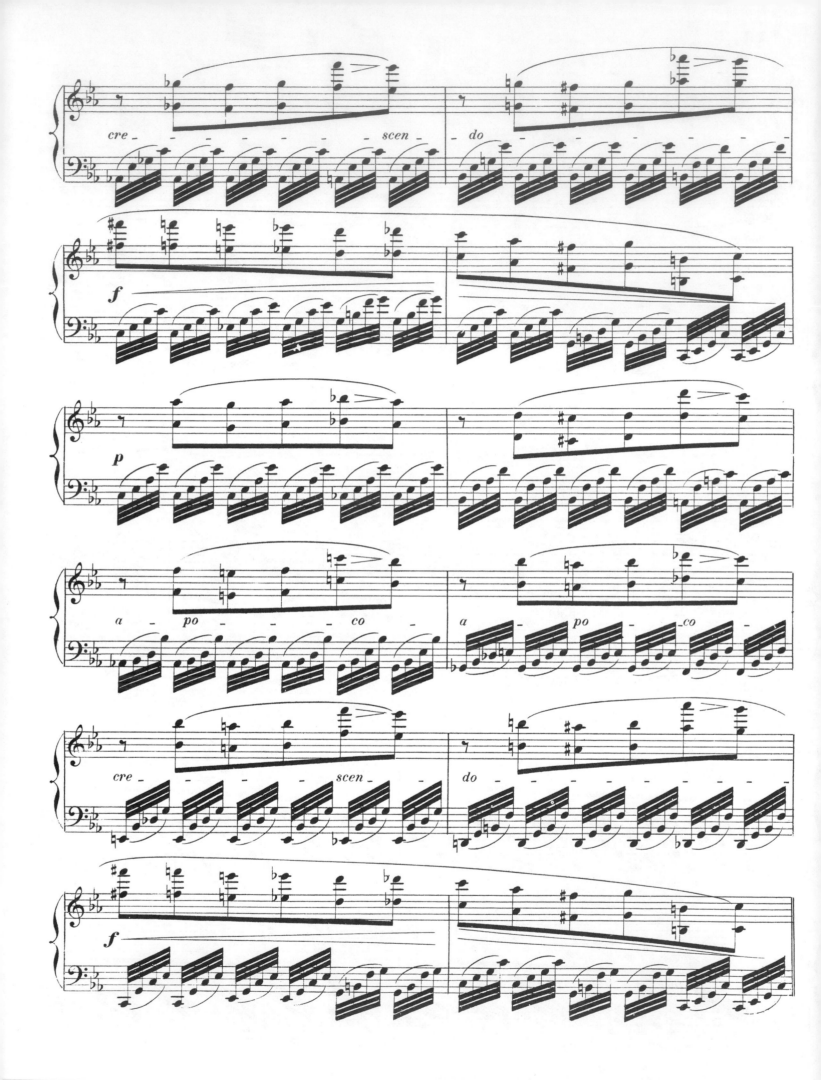

VAR. 9.
Un peu plus vite.

leggierissimo.
pp

pp

un peu plus vite: a little faster

VAR.10.

Alla Polacca.

staccato.

aussi *pp* que possible: as *pp* as possible

Plus animé: More lively

Mouvt. des Ires Variations: Tempo of the first variations

CODA.

semplice.
pp

cre scen do

-*f*

ff

Un peu plus lent.
melanconico.

pp

long. **pp**

rit. _ e _ dim. _ molto.

Ped. ✳

Quasi recitativo.

Un peu plus lent: A little more slowly

A. BORODINE. — PETITE SUITE

AU COUVENT

Nº 1

Andante religioso.

INTERMEZZO

N.º 2

Tempo di minuetto.

Alexander Borodin

MAZURKA

I

№ 3

Allegro.

Alexander Borodin

MAZURKA

II

N.º 4

Alexander Borodin

SÉRÉNADE

Alexander Borodin

NOCTURNE

№ 6

Ped. partout où les harmonies le permettent: Ped. wherever the harmonies permit

Alexander Borodin

RÊVERIE

N? 7

A Monsieur TH. JADOUL

SCHERZO

N°. 8

IMPROMPTU
POUR PIANO

à Madame Edouard MANET

Emmanuel CHABRIER

Pressez: Accelerate

presque sans mesure: practically disregarding the meter

à Louis DIÉMER

RONDE CHAMPÊTRE

POUR PIANO

EMMANUEL CHABRIER

Animato e leggieramente.

con delicatezza.

ritenuto.

Suite de quatre pièces.

C. Czerny. Op; 795, No 1.

Etude melodieuse.

C. Czerny. Op. 795.   Nº 3.

TOCCATA.

Allegro comodo. (♩ = 120.)

Carl Czerny

SONATA.

Op. 70.

LE RETOUR À PARIS.

Allegro non troppo ed espressivo.

Sonata "Le Retour à Paris": Allegro non troppo 171

Molto adagio con anima ed espressione.

Sonata "Le Retour à Paris": Molto adagio   177

Tempo di Menuetto. Scherzo quasi Allegro.

Jan Ladislav Dušek

FINALE.
Scherzo. Allegro con spirito.

Sonata "Le Retour à Paris": Finale   185

Sonata "Le Retour à Paris": Finale   189

190   Jan Ladislav Dusík

Sonata "Le Retour à Paris": Finale   191

J.

Anton Dvořák, Op. 8. Heft I.

Allegro feroce.

Allegretto grazioso.

Allegro feroce.

3.

Allegretto.

4.

Vivace.

Achtel wie früher Viertel: 8th-notes equal previous 4th-notes

Antonín Dvořák

5.

6.

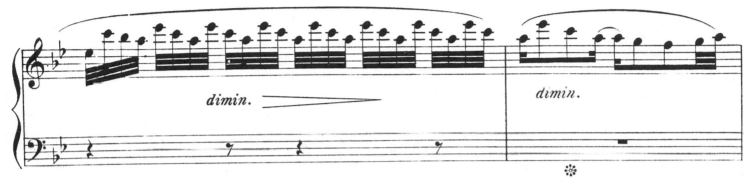

Antonín Dvořák

Thème et Variations.

Quasi adagio. (♩ = 50)

Gabriel Fauré, Op. 73.

PIANO.

Lo stesso tempo. ($\quarternote = 50$)

I.

dolce e sostenuto

Lo stesso tempo. (♩=104)

IV

Un poco più mosso. ($\dot{}$=116)

V.

Molto adagio. (♩=40)

VI.

VII.

Allegretto moderato. ($\bullet$ =69)

p legato espressivo

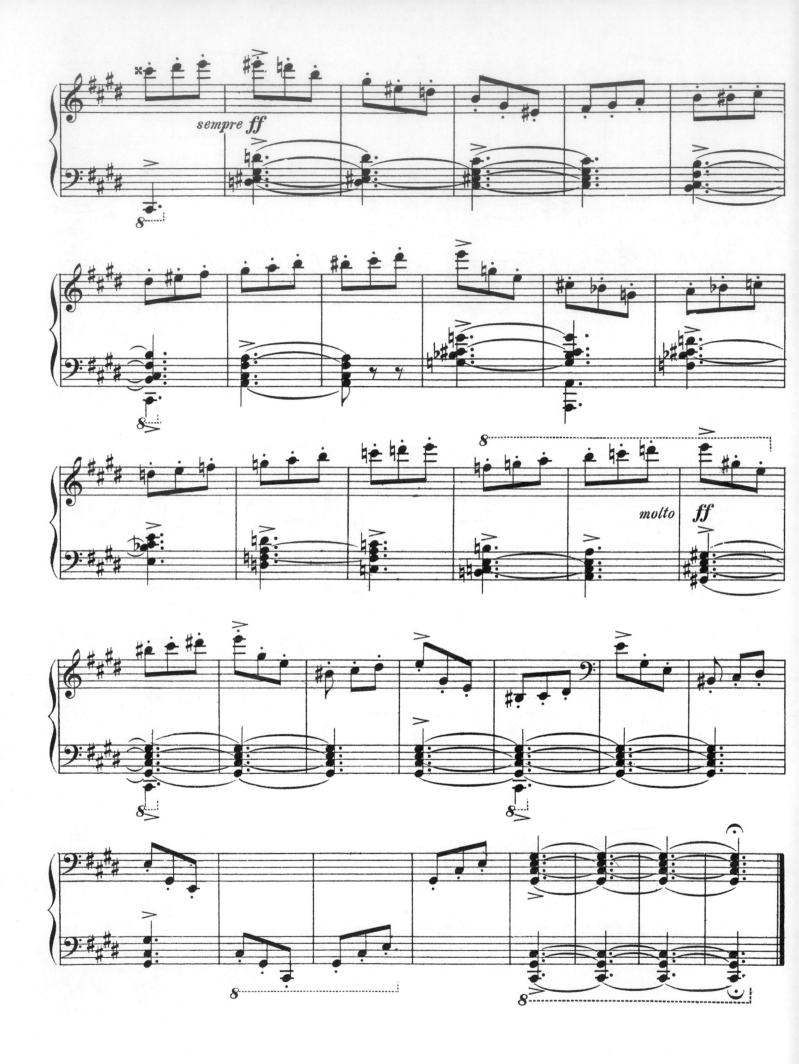

Poco adagio.

4.

Nocturne No. 4   233

I.

Revised and fingered by XAVER SCHARWENKA.

Niels W. Gade, Op. **27**.

III.

L'istesso tempo.

più vivo.

lento

IIII.

Allegretto grazioso.

IV.

I.

Enrique Granados

II.

RONDALLA ARAGONESA
VI.

Allegretto, poco a poco accelerando.

264   Enrique Granados

X.

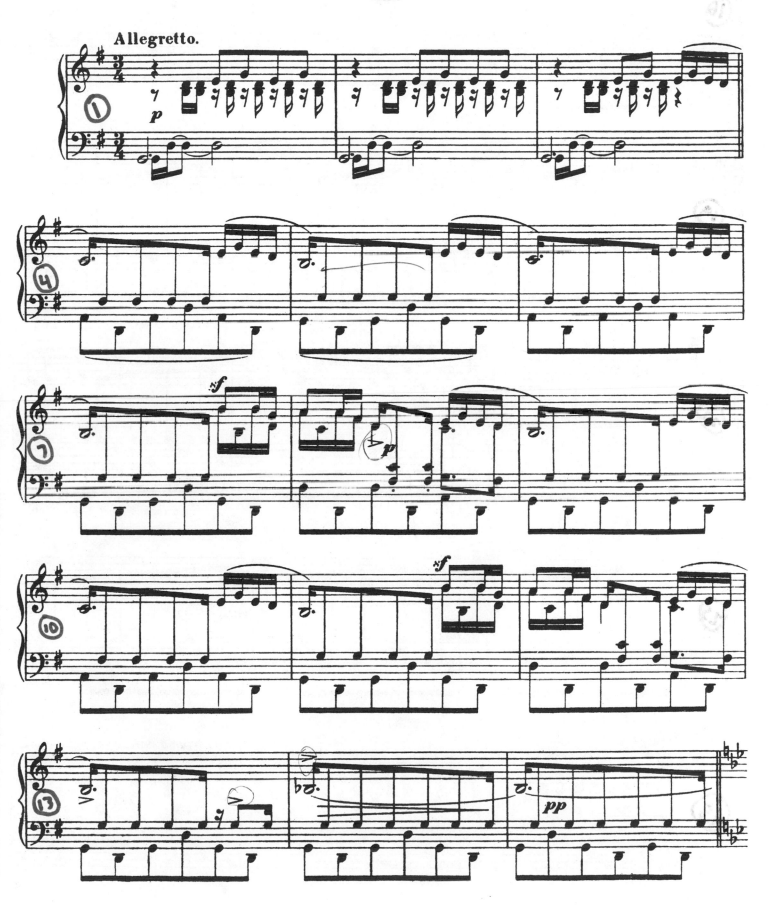

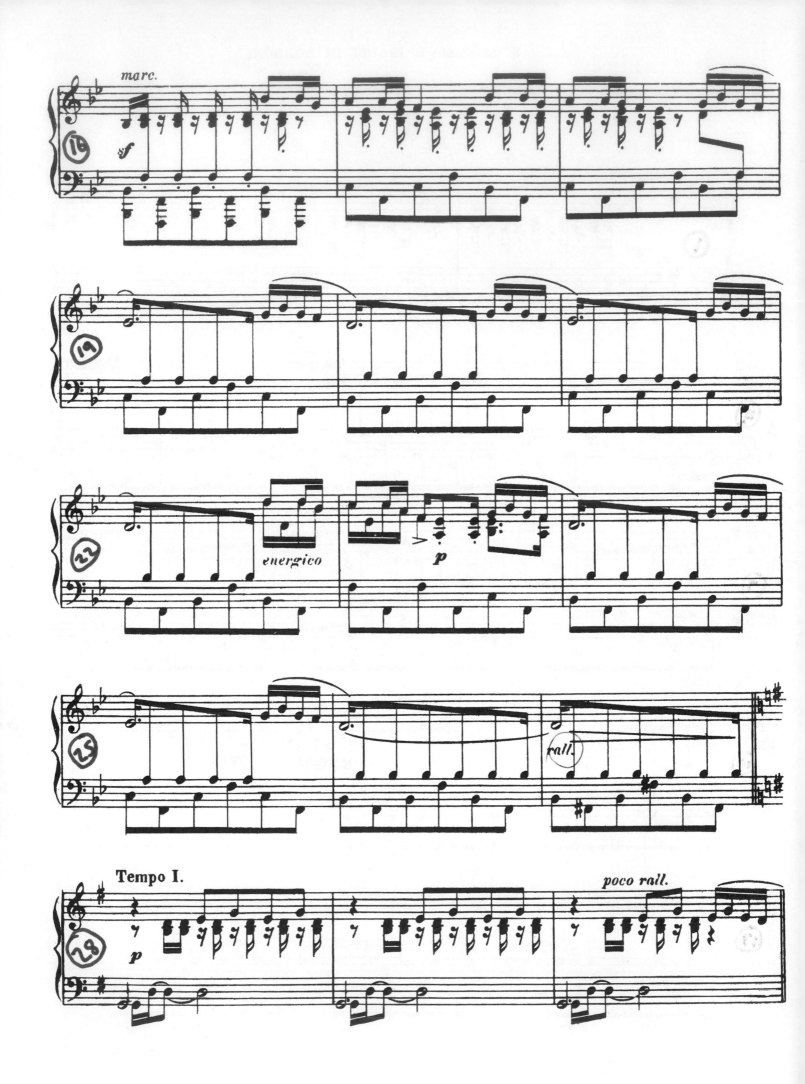

270   Enrique Granados

Drei deutsche Tänze.

I. Mässig.

PIANOFORTE.

Mässig: Moderate tempo

II. Bewegter.

III. Im selben Maasse.

Bewegter: More agitatedly   Im selben Maase: Same tempo

bis zum Schluss: to the end

D.C. bis zum Schluss.

STEPHAN HELLER.

Toccatina.

VAR.4.

Scherzando.

VAR.5.

VAR. 6.

VAR. 7.

VAR.8.

VAR.9.

Adagio espressivo.

La Forza.

Allegro con brio. M.M. ♩ = 138.

Risvegliato.

Polka poétique

Op. 8 Nr. 1
1855

VENKOVANKA

(1879)

Úvod: Introduction

Polka da Capo al signo ⊕ ed Coda

⊕ CODA

Auf stillem Waldespfad.

Dans le sentier silencieux de la forêt. In silent Forests.

Richard Strauss, Op. 9. N? 1.

Die Pedalzeichen sind sehr genau zu beobachten!
Les pédales doivent être observés rigoureusement.
Close attention should be paid to the pedal marks.

mit Wärme: with warmth

Intermezzo.

Richard Strauss, Op. 9. N<u>o</u> 3.

Die Pedalzeichen sind sehr genau zu beobachten!
Les pédales doivent être observés rigcureusement.
Close attention should be paid to the pedal marks.

TRE DITIRAMBI
per il Pianoforte
I.

VÁCLAV JAN TOMÁŠEK, Op. 65
(1774—1850)

ALBUM-SONATE.

RICHARD WAGNER.

Ruhig: Calmly

Ruhig wie vorher.

wie vorher: as previously   ausdrucksvoll: with expression
wie gesungen: cantabile

Von hier an sehr allmählich etwas bewegter im Vortrag und

Zeitmaass.

ausdrucksvoll.

Von hier an sehr . . . Zeitmaass: From here on, very gradually more agitated in execution
and tempo

Nach und nach wachsende Bewegung.

Nach und nach wachsende Bewegung: Gradually increasing agitation

immer bewegter: more and more agitatedly

Erstes Zeitmaass,

etwas zögernd.

Ped.

p

p

p

p

p

p zart.

3

3

p

3

3

p

p

zögernd.

p

cresc.

Erstes Zeitmaass: Tempo primo   etwas zögernd: somewhat hesitatingly
zart: gently

beruhigend: calming down

immer ruhiger: more and more calmly

Fine.